CHARISMATIC CONFUSION

CHARISMATIC CONFUSION

Updated and Expanded

Ernest D. Pickering

and

Myron J. Houghton

REGULAR BAPTIST PRESS
1300 North Meacham Road
Schaumburg, Illinois 60173-4806

CHARISMATIC CONFUSION
© 2006, 1980
Regular Baptist Press • Schaumburg, Illinois
www.regularbaptistpress.org • 1-800-727-4440
Printed in U.S.A.
All rights reserved
RBP5357 • ISBN: 978-1-59402-420-7

Contents

Charismatic Confusion in the 21st Century 7

Preface to the Updated Edition 9

The First Wave: Classical Pentecostalism 11

The Second Wave: The Charismatic Movement 15

The Third Wave: Signs and Wonders 19

Charismatic Confusion 23

Preface to the Original Edition 25

Exegetical Confusion 27

Dispensational Confusion 33

Theological Confusion 43

Ecclesiastical Confusion 49

Conclusion 57

Bibliography 59

CHARISMATIC CONFUSION IN THE 21ST CENTURY

Preface to the Updated Edition

I am honored that the editors at Regular Baptist Press have asked me to update the booklet entitled *Charismatic Confusion* written by my former theology professor, Dr. Ernest D. Pickering. It was published in 1976 by Baptist Bible College, Clarks Summit, Pennsylvania, and later published by Regular Baptist Press.

Rather than interrupting the flow of Dr. Pickering's work with my thoughts, I have chosen to provide this introductory update to the current charismatic scene and then to provide some current data for Dr. Pickering's original work.

In this update I intend to accomplish three goals.

First, I will sharpen the distinction between classical Pentecostalism (known as the "first wave" of the twentieth-century renewal of the gifts) and the charismatic movement (known as the "second wave"). A reference work that I found very helpful is *The New International Dictionary of Pentecostal and Charismatic Movements* (revised and expanded edition, Stanley M. Burgess, editor, Eduard M. van der Maas, associate editor; hereafter identified as NIDPCM).

Second, I will describe the "third wave," a movement that promotes and emphasizes "signs and wonders" but which did not exist at the time Dr. Pickering wrote his booklet.

Third, and finally, I will supplement each of the four major sections of Dr. Pickering's work with updated material.

These updates are found under the heading of "Confusion in the 21st Century" at the conclusion of each of Dr. Pickering's chapters.

The First Wave: Classical Pentecostalism

This movement began in the early 1900s among Wesleyan (or Holiness) people who believed God wanted to perform two works of grace in the life of a person: *salvation* in which one's sins were pardoned and a later work called *sanctification* in which the root of sin was replaced by intense love for God. For Wesleyans who had embraced Pentecostalism, speaking in tongues became the inevitable evidence of a third work of grace: the baptism of the Holy Spirit.

Generally when Holiness people began to speak in tongues, their denominations expelled them, and so they formed new organizations. Two such groups are the Church of God (Cleveland,

Tennessee) and the Pentecostal Holiness Church (since 1975 known as the International Pentecostal Holiness Church; NIDP-CM, 800).

Soon people from non-Wesleyan churches were speaking in tongues. They rejected the idea that believers could have the root of sin removed in an experience called sanctification. Instead they saw speaking in tongues as an evidence of the baptism of the Holy Spirit for power in growth and service. These people were known as "finished work" Pentecostals. The Assemblies of God denomination promotes this belief.

Another major theological division among early Pentecostals concerned the baptismal formula: Should one be baptized in the name of the Father, Son, and Holy Spirit, or in the name of Jesus Christ? Among those who argued for the latter formula were some who denied the triune nature of the Godhead, teaching instead the idea that there is only one Person in the Godhead. They believe Jesus is the name of the Father, Son, and Holy Spirit. Many of these people began to teach that water baptism in the name of Jesus, along with speaking in tongues, was necessary for the forgiveness of sins. The United Pentecostal Church advocates this view.

Classical Pentecostals taught that all of the gifts had been restored, and this included healing. They believed that Christ's death not only purchased forgiveness of sins but also healing for the body, and that believers have a right to claim both benefits. Support for faith healers like Kathryn Kuhlman and Oral Roberts has always been great. Another healing evangelist, Kenneth Hagin, Sr., has had a Pentecostal ministry since the late 1930s that has emphasized not only healing but prosperity as God's will for believers.

Characteristics of classical Pentecostalism include (1) a heritage originating in the early 1900s, (2) a strong emphasis on both personal and organizational separation, (3) a belief that security was conditional, thus salvation could be lost, and (4) an insistence that speaking in tongues was the necessary initial evidence of the baptism of the Holy Spirit. Usually the early Pentecostals were lower-income, blue-collar workers who had been marginalized by American society. Initially there was racial integration among these Pentecostals, but soon segregated church groups were formed.

The Second Wave: The Charismatic Movement

In the 1960s people in mainline liberal Protestant denominations, as well as people in the Catholic Church, began to speak in tongues. These people did not separate from their denominations but formed renewal groups within them. In contrast to classical Pentecostals, charismatics did not develop a well-defined theology but integrated their new experience with the doctrine of their denominations. Nor, for the most part, did charismatics change their lifestyles to conform to classical Pentecostal standards of godliness.

New organizations were created and new alignments were forged. Oral Roberts left the Pentecostal Holiness Church and joined the United Methodist Church. At the same time he founded Oral Roberts University. Lines of both organizational and personal separation were broken down between classical Pentecostals and mainline denominational charismatics, largely through the efforts of the Full Gospel Businessmen's Fellowship International (FGBFI). This group started in the early 1950s within classical Pentecostalism. Oral Roberts was the speaker for the first FGBFI meeting (NIDPCM, 653). The FGBFI used its meetings and its monthly publication, the *FGBFI Voice,* to report how Catholics, Episcopalians, Lutheran, Methodists, and other mainline Protestants were speaking in tongues.

David Du Plessis (1905–1987) was born and brought up in South Africa but later moved to the United States. Known as "Mr. Pentecost," he worked with several Pentecostal groups and by 1955 was ordained to minister in the Assemblies of God denomination. He was also known by some as the father of the charismatic movement. He promoted the charismatic experience at the World Council of Churches and at major nonconservative seminaries, such as Yale Divinity School, Union Theological Seminary in New York City, and Princeton Seminary. In 1962 he was forced to give up his credentials as an Assemblies of God minister. In 1980 those credentials were returned to him, showing the change in the separation emphasis in the Assemblies of God (NIDPCM, 589–593).

One ministry identified with the charismatic movement is Pat Robertson's television broadcast, *The 700 Club.* His school, Regent University in Virginia Beach, Virginia, is fully accredited. J. Rodman Williams, United Presbyterian renewal theologian, teaches there.

Paul Crouch is the founder and president of the Trinity Broadcasting Network (TBN). This network can be viewed throughout the United States and by satellite internationally. It has programs by evangelicals but promotes programming that is charismatic and that features prosperity preaching.

Many independent ministries centered around individuals and their distinctive emphases have sprung up within the charismatic movement. Prosperity preaching, for example, has been popularized by Kenneth Copeland, who studied at Oral Roberts University and attended seminars by Kenneth Hagin. He promotes his message through books and television programs. Other preachers who have been identified with prosperity teaching include Creflo Dollar, Frederick K. C. Price, and Jesse Duplantis. A book that proved helpful to me that critiqued the modern "faith" movement is *A Different Gospel* by D. R. McConnell.

The Third Wave: Signs and Wonders

Signs and wonders characterize the third wave. The signs and wonders associated with the ministry of Jesus receive special emphais: healing, the casting out of demons, and revelational messages about people (John 4:18, "Thou hast had five husbands; and he whom thou now hast is not thy husband").

John Wimber, a noted leader in the third wave movement, was greatly influenced by George Eldon Ladd, New Testament professor at Fuller Seminary. Ladd strongly opposed a dispensational understanding that the kingdom offered by John the Baptist and Jesus was rejected and postponed. To Ladd, the kingdom of God was the rule of God in one's heart and was, in fact, being established wherever the gospel was being proclaimed. Ladd's view was foundational to Wimber's ministry. In his book *Power Evangelism,* John Wimber says, "I am also thankful for the late George Ladd, whose pioneering work on the kingdom of God forms the theological foundation for power evangelism" (xiii). Wimber's third wave organization is known as the Vineyard movement. Following Ladd's view of prophecy, the Vineyard movement is posttribulational in its view of the Rapture.

A fascinating history of the Vineyard movement is *The Quest for the Radical Middle* by Bill Jackson. This book shows Wimber's early connection with Chuck Smith's Calvary Chapel movement. Differences over how prominent the gifts should be and whether or not believers today will go through the Tribulation helped bring about a parting of ways between Wimber and Smith.

C. Peter Wagner, who coined the term "third wave," taught at Fuller Seminary and actively worked with Wimber. Wagner's distinctive emphasis is on the reestablishment of apostles for today. He stated, "Back in the 1990s we began hearing the Holy Spirit speaking about restoring apostles and prophets as the foundation of the church as God originally designed." Wagner identifies himself as "the Presiding Apostle over" the International Coalition of Apostles. You can learn more about his views on his Web site: http://www.globalharvest.org.

The Kansas City Prophets emphasized the revelational gifts and for a while were identified with the Vineyard movement, but extreme pronouncements caused the group to separate. From 1993 until August 2000, C. Samuel Storms was identified with the Kansas City Prophets. In the book *Are Miraculous Gifts For Today? Four Views,* Storms defends the third wave view.

The Toronto Blessing centered around the Vineyard church in Toronto, but extreme demonstrations of laughing and barking like a dog caused the Vineyard leadership to break their ties. See Hank Hanegraaff's critical article, "The Counterfeit Revival, Part One:

Rodney Howard-Browne and the Toronto Blessing" (*Christian Research Journal*, 8–18).

A book that analyzes the Vineyard movement is *Strange Fire?* by Eric E. Wright. This book is especially helpful because it evaluates not only the Vineyard movement but also the Kansas City Prophets and the Toronto Blessing.

Wayne Grudem has also been identified with the third wave movement, primarily because of his emphasis that the New Testament gift of prophecy exists today. Grudem's book, *The Gift of Prophecy in the New Testament and Today,* was reviewed from a cessationist viewpoint (i.e., sign gifts have ceased) in an excellent fourteen-page article by Robert L. Thomas (*Bibliotheca Sacra*, 83–96).

Characteristics of the third wave movement include the following: (1) tongues occur today but are not emphasized; rather healing, exorcism, and revelational messages are prominent; (2) many adherents do not hold the Pentecostal or charismatic view that speaking in tongues is connected to Spirit baptism; (3) many are Calvinistic in their doctrine of salvation, believing in the eternal security of the believer.

The Brownsville, Florida, revival (Assembly of God in Pensacola) involved unusual demonstrations of fervor that really do not fit neatly into any of the three wave categories. See Hank Hanegraaff's critical article, "The Counterfeit Revival, Part Three: Separating Fact from Fabrication on the Pensalcola Outpouring" in *Christian Research Journal* (11–20, 42).

CHARISMATIC CONFUSION

Preface to the Original Edition

Few subjects are as hotly disputed in current Christendom as the subject of the "gift of tongues." In the last few years the so-called "charismatic movement" has swept the world, infiltrating most denominations and many independent Christian groups as well. Celebrated personalities are paraded as recipients of the gift. Tremendous stress is laid upon the importance of special spiritual gifts, particularly the gift of tongues. For many years this emphasis was found primarily in smaller, fringe groups not considered to be a part of the historic stream of conservative Christianity. However, more recently charismatics have become prominent in many different denominational and undenominational organizations. The rise of the charismatic movement has been hailed as a sign of a great spiritual awakening within the church. While the emphasis in the popular mind is upon the gift of tongues, many charismatics are claiming a revival of other gifts as well.

What is meant by the term "charismatic"? In general, as commonly used today, it refers to people who believe that the gift of tongues spoken of in the New Testament is still being bestowed by God today, is an important gift, and should be exercised in the churches. Many, if not most, charismatics also believe that other spiritual gifts, long thought by most conservative Bible expositors to be inoperative today in the church, are being divinely bestowed and ought to be used. Among these would be such gifts as prophecy, healing, and the working of miracles. The term itself is derived from the Greek word *charisma,* generally rendered by the English word "gift" (as in Romans 12:6).

The charismatic movement is a result of exegetical, dispensational, and theological confusion. This confusion then affects church groups and denominations.

Exegetical Confusion

Exegesis is the science of determining the meaning of the original text of Scripture. Much of the confusion of the charismatic movement stems from a failure to properly understand certain key passages, phrases, and words of the Bible.

The Meaning of *Glossa*

Glossa is the word in the New Testament for "tongue." The unfortunate insertion of an English word not found in the original Biblical text has contributed to the misunderstanding of the usage of the word "tongue." A sample of this is found in 1 Corinthians 14:2 where the translation states, "for he that speaketh in an *unknown* tongue speaketh not unto men, but unto God." The fact that the word "unknown" is there (even though some charismatics understand it is not valid) nevertheless lends credence in the popular mind to the concept that what is described is some mysterious, heavenly, or unintelligible utterance.

Actually, the word *glossa* refers to a spoken language, not communication foreign to common human experience. (It, of course, sometimes refers to that portion of the human anatomy with which we speak.) The first mention in the New Testament of a "gift of tongues" is found in Acts 2:1–13. The waiting believers "began to speak with other tongues, as the Spirit gave them utterance" (v. 4). What were these tongues with which they spoke? It is plainly stated in the following passage that "every man heard them speak in his own language" (v. 6). They asked, "How hear we every man in our own tongue, wherein we were born?" (v. 8). It is clear from this passage that the gift bestowed on the Day of Pentecost was the supernatural and instantaneous ability to preach the gospel of Christ in a language naturally foreign to the user.

There are those who argue for a distinction between tongues-speaking in Acts 2 and in 1 Corinthians. The former is made to be intelligent communication while the latter is said to have been ecstatic utterances or "heavenly languages." However, as John F. Walvoord notes in his discussion of this matter, there is really no foundation grammatically which would justify a distinction to be made. The passages in Acts and 1 Corinthians use the same words for "speaking" and for "tongue" (*The Holy Spirit*, 183).

The Significance of 1 Corinthians 14:39

Those who oppose the validity of the gift of tongues today are often made to seem in opposition to the statement of Paul, "Wherefore, brethren, covet to prophesy, and forbid not to speak with tongues" (1 Cor. 14:39). Did not Paul admonish us to allow people to speak with tongues? Why should we then seek to prevent them? The answer to this question is evident upon an examination of all of the evidence. (1) This prohibition was addressed to the early Christians living in the Apostolic Age. (2) When the command was given, the gift of tongues was still being bestowed upon some believers for the fulfillment of God's purposes at that time. (3) The words were penned prior to the time when certain miraculous gifts ceased. At that time it would have been wrong for anyone to interfere with the proper exercise of the divinely bestowed gift of tongues. Today the use of tongues should be forbidden because it is no longer a divinely bestowed gift. Any claimed gift of tongues is spurious and should be prohibited by the churches of Christ.

The Significance of 1 Corinthians 13:8–10

In the great thirteenth chapter of 1 Corinthians, Paul asserted the fact that love is permanent, whereas special sign gifts such as prophecy, tongues, and knowledge are temporary. "Charity [love] never faileth" (1 Cor. 13:8). The others shall "fail" (that is, disappear). The word literally means "to fall."

Paul specifically declared, "Whether there be tongues, they shall cease" (1 Cor. 13:8). What did he mean by this? When would tongues cease? Some good Bible expositors believe that the reference is to the end of the age, the coming of Christ, when we shall be glorified. Those who hold this view generally believe that the phrase "when that which is perfect is come" (1 Cor. 13:10) refers to that future state of glorification with Christ. They would thus feel that, from this passage at least, it would be impossible to prove the complete cessation of miraculous gifts such as tongues during the Church Age.

However, a close look at the entire passage seems to indicate that Paul's argument flows in a somewhat different vein. First of all, he declared that there are some methods of revelation that were partial and temporary in nature. The three special gifts mentioned—prophecy, tongues, and knowledge—are all stated to be temporary and are predicted to discontinue (1 Cor. 13:8). These methods of revelation were partial in nature. They were given to the early churches during the interim period when the New Testament was not yet completed and available. This partial and incomplete revelation is in view in verse 9, "For we know in part, and we prophesy in part." The phrase "in part" means "imperfectly, incompletely, piece by piece, little by little." Prophecy was a gift that involved receiving special and direct revelation from God in order to give it to His people. It was exercised here and there, at different times and places. Knowledge was the ability to receive direct spiritual truth. This truth would later be found in the New Testament, but as yet was not recorded because the books were still in the process of being written. Tongues as a gift was directly connected by the apostle with these other two. They formed a part of the method by which God communicated truth during a time when believers had no written New Testament. In other words, tongues were never intended to be a permanent fixture within the New Testament church. They were part of a temporary arrangement.

Having spoken of temporary and partial revelation, Paul then contrasted it with the permanent and complete revelation of the Scriptures. The phrase "that which is perfect" (1 Cor. 13:10) means "the final thing, the completed thing." Neither the context nor the language would seem to support the concept that Paul referred to Heaven or the future glorified state. The phrase is the culmination of a logical argument, moving from temporary and partial revelation to permanent and complete revelation. Revelation is the key thought, not glorification.

If this be the case, then the phrase "tongues shall cease" is very important in the present consideration. We would agree with Merrill Unger who concludes that the Greek text of 1 Corinthians 13:8 contains a strong affirmation of the temporary character of at least three gifts—prophecy, tongues, and knowledge (*New Testament Teaching on Tongues*, p. 95).

Exegetical Confusion in the 21st Century

Dr. Pickering said that charismatics misunderstand certain passages or words found in the Bible. First, tongues in Acts is the same as tongues in 1 Corinthians. In "Appendix 5: Were New Testament Tongues Real Languages?" of *Signs and Wonders,* Norman Geisler argues in the affirmative, showing that the Greek word for tongues in Acts is the same word used in 1 Corinthians and that the word "unknown" found in some English versions before "tongues" is not found in any Greek text but was added by the translators (165–168).

Second, concerning the use of 1 Corinthians 14:39, "Forbid not to speak with tongues," Dr. Pickering pointed to 1 Corinthians 13:8–10 to show that Paul had previously said that tongues, prophecy, and knowledge were temporary. Pickering argued that Paul's admonition in 1 Corinthians 14:39 was meant only during the interim. Dr. Pickering believed that prophecy, tongues, and knowledge gave partial revelation, but when the revelation was completed, these gifts communicating partial revelation were no longer necessary and thus came to an end. This writer (Myron Houghton) agrees and points the reader to his article in *Bibliotheca Sacra* for a detailed defense. See "A Reexamination of 1 Corinthians 13:8–13" by Myron J. Houghton (344–356).

Dispensational Confusion

By "dispensation" we mean a period of time during which God tests man in reference to some specific revelation of His will. Failure to recognize various dispensations, or special, distinct methods of divine operation, can cause confusion in Biblical interpretation. For example, those who equate the nation Israel with the church and view the church as "spiritual Israel" evidence confusion in their understanding of many passages of Scripture. It seems clear in the New Testament that the gift of tongues was given for a particular period of time and not for the entire Church Age.

When argument is made against the perpetuation of the gift of tongues, the question is sometimes asked, "Are we not limiting God when we say He cannot grant such a gift today? Is not God able to do anything? Can He not sovereignly bestow the gift of tongues upon whom He will?"

The answer to such a question is clear. God is omnipotent, all-powerful. But there are some things God cannot and will not do. He will not sin because to do so would be a violation of His holy character. He is "limited" in this case by His own nature. God could instantly stop all conflict among nations, but prophetic Scripture declares He will not do so at this time. Why? He is "limited" by His own purposes. It is not the time in His program for wars to cease. His failure to act reveals no lack of power on His part.

So it is with the gift of tongues. While theoretically God could bestow any spiritual gift He wished, He does not and will not do so in contradiction to His revealed purposes. He has declared in His Word that the gift of tongues would cease; it would be bestowed no longer. He is "limited" by His own plan not by lack of sovereign power.

The Perpetuation of Sign Gifts

Many modern charismatics not only accept the gift of tongues as valid for today, but they see all of the gifts mentioned in the New Testament as still in use (for example, the discussion on "The Further Gifts of the Spirit" in *The Holy Spirit in Today's Church* edited by Erling Jorstad). In other words, they argue that the spiritual gifts practiced in the early church should be practiced today, though most adherents place more emphasis upon the gift of tongues than some of the other gifts.

Did God intend for all the gifts mentioned in Ephesians 4, Romans 12, and 1 Corinthians 12—14 to be perpetuated throughout the Church Age? Are we evidencing a backslidden, disobedient, and spiritually cold condition by our failure to see all of these gifts utilized in our churches? The New Testament gives ample evidence that God never intended for all of these gifts to continue throughout the entire Church Age.

Some gifts were for the time of incomplete revelation.
It has already been noted in 1 Corinthians 13 that Paul argued for the temporary nature of some gifts. After the completion of the New Testament canon, these gifts would cease.

Some gifts were for the time of the church's childhood.
In arguing for the temporary character of certain gifts, including tongues, Paul used the illustration of physical and mental growth from childhood to adulthood. Why did he use this illustration? He wished to show that the church was in a process of development at the time he wrote—from infancy to maturity. "Progressive development from infancy to maturity in Paul's personal life would best suit the development of the body of Christ (cf. 1 Cor. 12)" (Robert Gromacki, *The Modern Tongues Movement*, 127). Language, thoughts, and actions that characterize an infant do not evidence themselves in a grownup. Gifts such as tongues, which were practiced in the infancy of the church, were not appropriate for its maturity.

Some gifts were divine signs attesting to the truthfulness of the apostolic witness.
The apostles of Christ came into the Roman Empire and into Jewish communities preaching a startling message. They were declaring that the crucified Jesus of Nazareth had been miraculously raised from the dead, that He had ascended to Heaven, and that He was the promised Messiah and the only Savior of all men. This was a very difficult announcement for either Jew or Gentile to receive. What proof was there that this Jesus was Messiah and Savior? How could men know that what the apostles preached was accurate? God solved this problem by granting to the apostles

and other early Christians supernatural abilities, mighty signs, that served to corroborate the truthfulness of their message.

The apostles were men especially called and gifted of God for the purpose of laying the foundation of the church (Eph. 2:20). The very fact that they are described in such a way indicates that their gift was a temporary one. Foundations are laid and then the superstructure is built upon them. Once the foundation was completed, the apostolic gift was removed. "Since this was a gift that belonged to the earliest period of the history of the church when her foundation was being laid, the need for the gift has ceased" (Charles Ryrie, *The Holy Spirit*, 85).

So, if the gift of apostleship was temporary, and if that gift was attested by other special gifts, the necessity for these attesting gifts no longer exists. In other words, if special gifts were given as "signs" that an apostle of Christ was working and speaking, and if there are no more apostles of Christ, then it seems evident that the special signs that accompanied their ministry are no longer operative either. We are expressly told that there were such special gifts. In arguing for the importance of the apostolic message, the writer of Hebrews declares that God set forth the apostles so everyone would know they were from God. "God also bearing them witness, both with signs and wonders, and with divers miracles, and gifts of the Holy Ghost, according to his own will" (Heb. 2:4).

Miraculous signs were performed in New Testament times to bear witness to the divine source of the apostolic message. We should not expect such signs to be seen today because there are no apostles. The same truth is found in 2 Corinthians 12:12: "Truly the signs of an apostle were wrought among you in all patience, in signs, and wonders, and mighty deeds." As Charles Hodge, the eminent theologian stated, "The signs of an apostle were the insignia of the apostleship; those things which by divine appointment were made the evidence of a mission from God" (*An*

Exposition of the Second Epistle to the Corinthians, 290–91).

The question remains, if the apostleship were temporary, and if the special sign gifts attesting the apostleship were temporary, was the gift of tongues one of these gifts? It seems clear from 1 Corinthians 14:22 that it was. Paul argued that "tongues are for a sign." The exact purpose of that sign we shall discover in a further discussion. However, the gift was definitely a "sign," an outward, miraculous, visible authentication of a divinely sent person and/or his message. Since the gift of tongues was included among the signs accompanying the preaching and ministry of the apostles, and since there are no apostles today, it follows that the signs that accompanied them are no longer present either.

The Purpose of the Tongues Gift
The charismatic claims

The crux of the conflict over the validity of the gift of tongues is settled right here. For what purpose was the gift originally given? Most present-day advocates of tongues give answers such as: (1) it is the visible sign of the baptism of the Holy Spirit; or (2) it enables recipients to pray, give thanks, and worship God in a more satisfying manner.

For the moment we will bypass the question of the alleged connection between the baptism of the Spirit and speaking in tongues, reserving this for a later discussion. We will concentrate on the question of whether or not the gift of tongues was ever intended to be devotional in nature since this is a favorite contention of modern charismatics.

One leading Pentecostal author declares that "the chief purpose of tongues is to provide the human spirit with an opportunity to worship God in ecstatic prayer, praise, thanksgiving, and song" (Carl Brumback, *What Meaneth This?* 303). If one speaks in tongues, it is claimed, one can praise God so much better. Why one cannot praise God adequately in one's native language is not abundantly clear. At any rate, the so-called "devotional use" of tongues is prominent on the charismatic scene at present.

Is it God's intention that believers be privately edified by speaking in tongues? Those who think so rest their case primarily upon a few verses in 1 Corinthians. For instance, Paul states, "He that speaketh in an unknown tongue edifieth himself; but he that prophesieth edifieth the church" (1 Cor. 14:4). This, however, is not an exhortation to private edification through tongues, but an argument by Paul to the effect that tongues were not intended for private use but for public ministry, and that tongues-speaking is less desirable than prophesying. Likewise, in 1 Corinthians 14:14 Paul wrote, "For if I pray in an unknown tongue, my spirit prayeth, but my understanding is unfruitful." This verse, combined with verse 15, is often used by charismatics to argue in favor of tongues as a devotional exercise. However, as Hoekema notes, the subject here is not the private exercise but the use of tongues in public services. In 1 Corinthians 14:15 Paul was not expressing favor toward the use of tongues either publicly or privately, but rather was pleading the superiority of praying in a known language (Anthony Hoekema, *What about Tongue Speaking?* 100).

Why must we reject the concept that the purpose of the gift of tongues was to enable private praise and thanksgiving to God? First of all, this concept militates against the express statement of Scripture that the gift was intended as a sign (as in Mark 16:17). If a "sign," then it must be exercised publicly in order to have its intended effect. Private usage would hardly fulfill this purpose. Second, there is no evidence that the early Christians employed the gift of tongues privately. Third, Paul's argument in 1 Corinthians 14 is not intended to show that one can have a better devotional life through the use of tongues. He plainly stated that it is better to worship God with one's spirit and understanding than in a tongue (1 Cor. 14:14, 15). Fourth, we need to ask, if the purpose of the gift were devotional in nature, why would it be temporary? Why would it not be continued throughout the Church Age?

Scriptural teaching

What then was the purpose for which God bestowed the gift of tongues? The specific answer can be found in 1 Corinthians 14:20–22. As one has said, "It is within this passage that there is to be found the only direct and specific Scriptural statement regarding the purpose of the gift of tongues" (Zane Hodges, "The Purpose of Tongues," *Bibliotheca Sacra,* 228). Let us examine this vital statement.

The prophet Isaiah foretold a time when God would specially and specifically speak to the nation Israel. "For with stammering lips and another tongue will he speak to this people" (Isa. 28:11). Israel often did not listen in obedience to the Old Testament prophets who proclaimed to them the Word of the Lord. Isaiah foretold the time when the nation would hear his voice through the medium of "tongues." Paul, in citing this verse, gave us the key to the understanding of tongues. It was a gift meant to be a special sign to the nation Israel that Christ and His apostles were sent from God and should be heeded. The explanation of the events of Pentecost by the apostle Peter seem to support the conclusion that tongues was a divinely intended sign to the nation Israel.

> Therefore being by the right hand of God exalted, and having received of the Father the promise of the Holy Ghost, he hath shed forth this [the supernatural manifestation of the Spirit and its evidence of tongues], which ye now see and hear. . . . Therefore let all the house of Israel know assuredly, that God hath made that same Jesus, whom ye have crucified, both Lord and Christ (Acts 2:33–36).

How was Israel "to know assuredly" that Christ was the Messiah and that the apostles preached the truth? Because they saw and heard "this": remarkable and predicted manifestation of tongues. Paul specifies that the sign was to the unbelieving (1 Cor. 14:22) and to "this people," the nation Israel to whom the original prophesied words were given (1 Cor. 14:21). "The scriptural testimony bears sufficient witness to the fact that the ability to speak in other tongues (languages) vindicated and authenticated both the messenger and his message to the nation Israel" (Robert Lightner, *Speaking in Tongues and Divine Healing*, 28).

❖

Dispensational Confusion in the 21st Century

Wayne Grudem, who identifies himself as charismatic, agrees with Dr. Pickering's statement that charismatics "not only accept the gift of tongues as valid for today, but see all of the gifts mentioned in the New Testament as still in use." He says, "Charismatic, on the other hand, refers to any groups (or people) that trace their historical origin to the charismatic renewal movement of the 1960s and 1970s and that seek to practice all the spiritual gifts mentioned in the New Testament (including prophecy, healing, miracles, tongues, interpretation, and distinguishing between spirits)." See *Are Miraculous Gifts For Today? Four Views,* Wayne Grudem, general editor (11).

Dr. Pickering indicated that with the death and resurrection of Christ and the coming of the Holy Spirit at Pentecost, God was no longer offering Israel an earthly kingdom; He had begun a new program with a new group: the church. The book of Acts, then, describes an interim period in which the old program is declared closed and the new program is inaugurated. For a presentation from this perspective see, "Did Jesus Correct the Disciples' View of the Kingdom?" by John A. McLean (*Bibliotheca Sacra,* 215–227).

In developing this theme, Dr. Pickering showed that some gifts were for the time of incomplete revelation, some gifts were for the time of the church's childhood, and some gifts were signs from God attesting to the truthfulness of the witness of the apostles. It is at this point that he showed from Ephesians 2:20 that apostles are to be found only in the foundational stage of the church, and he argued that the gifts attesting to the validity of the apostles' ministry passed away when the apostles passed from the scene. It is interesting to note that in 2001 the General Presbytery of the Assemblies of God, a Pentecostal denomination, officially adopted a position paper that clearly states the office of apostle in a technical sense ended with the death of the original apostles. "The statement *Apostles and Prophets* was adopted as the official statement by the General Presbytery of the Assemblies of God on August 6, 2001." See the Assemblies of God Web site http://ag.org. (Follow the link to "beliefs" and click on "position papers.")

Theological Confusion

Theology, the systematic study of God and His works, is vital to the spiritual life of an individual believer as well as to the collective testimony of the church. The Pentecostal, or charismatic, movement historically has not been noted for its emphasis upon theology. There is some interest in the study of theology among current neo-Pentecostals, but basically it has been an experience-centered movement.

The Emphasis upon Experience

It is interesting that Morton Kelsey, a leading spokesman for the charismatic movement, has subtitled his major work, *Encounter With God,* as *A Theology of Christian Experience.* Throughout the study he places great emphasis upon one's *experience* with God. The word "experience" is employed scores of times. He declares that the early church was experiential in its primary outlook. He further encourages the "inward look" if one would be used of God. He believes the Spirit-filled life to be "mysticism," and he hastens to add that it is evidenced by speaking in tongues (Morton Kelsey, *Encounter With God*, 154, 157, 165).

This emphasis upon the inward, upon feeling, upon religious mysticism is typical of the charismatic movement. Its practical outworking is seen when one endeavors to present Biblical theological truth that is opposed to the charismatic claims only to receive the retort, "Oh, but you've never experienced it. I've felt it, and it's so wonderful!" One's Christian life, however, ought not to be built upon feelings, however good they may seem, but upon the rock of Holy Scripture. We would agree with the analysis of another who wrote:

> A tongues speaker recently wrote the editor of *Christianity Today*, "You cannot give fair treatment to a gift from God which you neither believe in or have experienced." This person has really said that tongues speaking is not subject to critical examination in the light of Scripture. Yet to say that the one who has spoken in tongues is the only one qualified to comment on the subject is to assume the experience is a gift of God and to put the subjective above the Scripture.
>
> Since what has happened to the glossolalist is no more exempt from the judgment of the Word of God than any other aspect of the Christian life, the tongues speaker should be willing to examine his experience in the light of Scripture. Only in this way can he determine whether or not his experience is the same as that spoken of as tongues in the New Testament. (Stanley Gundry, "Facing the Issue of Tongues," *Moody Monthly*, 96)

One can scarcely believe the extreme statements made when emphasizing "experience." An example is found in Christenson's work where he argues that the Christian faith is basically an "experience" and theology is merely an explanation of the experience (Larry Christenson, "How to Have a Daily Quiet Time with God," *Speaking in Tongues,* 136). The same author in another place says that speaking in tongues means praying in the Spirit rather than with the mind and further teaches that by praying in tongues one can bypass the intellect (Christenson, 73). This emphasis upon experience is completely contrary to the teachings of the New Testament. Our minds are to be very active in the proper worship of God.

The Nature of the Spirit's Baptism

Pentecostalism and Neo-Pentecostalism center in large measure around the doctrine of the Holy Spirit's baptism. Typically they would view the baptism of the Spirit as taking place at a definite time and as being a "conscious experience." (As an example, see Bob E. Patterson, "Catholic Pentecostals," in the book *Speaking in Tongues; Let's Talk about It,* edited by Watson Mills, 105.)

Let us examine that claim. The determinative passage is 1 Corinthians 12:13. There the baptism of the Spirit is stated to be a sovereign work of the Spirit performed upon every believer. Nothing is said about it being a "conscious experience." In fact, it is not a "conscious experience," that is, something perceptible to the senses. It is an instantaneous and nonexperiential work of God.

Most modern charismatics distinguish between tongues as an *evidence* of the Spirit's baptism and tongues as a *gift* of the Holy Spirit (Carl Brumback, *What Meaneth This?* 261–272). Brumback and others who hold this position attempt to distinguish between the tongues of Acts and the tongues of 1 Corinthians. Suffice to say at this point that there is no Scripture in the New Testament that declares that speaking in tongues is an evidence of the baptism of the Holy Spirit. The misunderstanding has arisen due to the fact that in Acts 1:5 the baptizing work of the Spirit is predicted, and then in Acts 2:4 the waiting disciples are said to be "filled with the Holy Ghost," which was followed by their speaking in tongues. Since the term "baptized with the Holy Ghost" is employed in the prophecy of Acts 1:5 and since that same phrase does *not* appear in the account of Acts 2, but rather the "filling of the Holy Ghost" is mentioned, some have drawn the erroneous conclusion that the "baptism" and the "filling," are one and the same. They have also concluded that because the apostles spoke in tongues in connection with their "baptism" or "filling" every other believer will also do the same. This deduction, however, is not supported by a close examination of the Scriptures. Several considerations should be noted.

(1) The prediction of Acts 1:5 was fulfilled at Pentecost. The disciples were baptized by the Spirit. Acts 11:15–17 so indicates.

(2) The filling of the Spirit mentioned in Acts 2:4, however, was *not* a fulfillment of Acts 1:5. The baptism of the Spirit is a *once-for-all* ministry performed on behalf of *every* believer (1 Cor. 12:13). The filling of the Spirit is a *continuous* and contingent ministry performed with *some* believers who meet the conditions (Eph. 5:18).

(3) Speaking in tongues is not a necessary result of either the baptism or the filling. The key verses on these subjects show no necessary connection between either of these ministries and the gift of tongues (1 Cor. 12:13; Eph. 5:18).

It is most instructive that there is *no command in the New Testament for anyone to be baptized with the Spirit.* There is *no invitation for anyone to pray for the baptism of the Spirit.* These facts are sufficient in themselves to sound the death knell of the charismatic movement. There are no such commands or invitations because the Holy Spirit baptizes all believers the moment they are saved, placing them into the body of Christ. The believer has nothing to seek or to do. It is done by God alone.

The Importance of the Gift of Tongues

Modern charismatics place far more importance upon the gift of tongues than did even the apostles when the gift was operative. One of Paul's principal arguments in 1 Corinthians 14 is that tongues was a relatively minor gift. There were other gifts far more significant. The constant glorification of tongues in the public eye that has been done by the charismatics is completely out of touch with what the New Testament presents.

❖

Theological Confusion in the 21st Century

Dr. Pickering critiqued those who promote the sign gifts for their emphasis on experience. In looking for material to update this criticism, I went to Amazon.com and typed in "Charismatic Confusion." To my amazement Amazon listed Dr. Pickering's booklet. If you have ever found a book at that site, you know that often a reader will review it. And, yes, there was a review of Dr. Pickering's booklet. I quote the review in full.

> There's no confusion at all if you know what the Word says. The only truly confused people are the ones involved with powerless religion and serving the god of their imagination and their tradition. Powerless religion says that "miracles aren't for today" and basically that everything but not going to hell "passed away with the apostles." Powerless religion blames God for sickness, problems, and calamity. Powerless religion always accuses God's true servants of being "of the devil." Powerless religion specializes in behavior modification and condemnation. Powerless religion causes people to judge others rather than themselves. Powerless religion comes up with terms like "tongue-talkers" and "demon tongues," instead of realizing that

God's Word says praying in other tongues magnifies God and builds us up on our most holy faith. Only a highly "educated" cemetery [sic] student would enjoy a book like this one. You need to repent before God and realize that you have been lied to. (Review by Christopher Thompson, September 10, 2005)

My response to this "review" is, What a wonderful example of Dr. Pickering's criticism that charismatics often place an inappropriate emphasis on experience. Thus, a "religion with power," rather than one with a detailed explanation of what the Bible teaches, becomes the basis for accepting or rejecting an idea.

Ecclesiastical Confusion

What effect has the charismatic movement had in the churches of this land and others?

The Charismatic Movement as an Ecumenical Catalyst

Certainly no movement of the twentieth century within the church has the potential for spanning denominational barriers as does the charismatic movement. In an age that hails all kinds of religious cooperation as good and progressive, the charismatic movement is being looked upon with delight by many. Virtually every traditional division of Christendom is found under the umbrella of what is called the "charismatic renewal." One leading proponent of the "renewal" believes it has ecumenical importance of great significance (Watson Mills, editor, *Speaking in Tongues: Let's Talk about It,* 13).

The phenomenon of tongues-speaking has gained a foothold in practically every major denomination. The old-line denominations whose leadership is dominated by liberals of various shades are infiltrated with charismatic persons who are either exercising their claimed gifts within the structure of the established churches or on their periphery in private gatherings.

Members of various denominations meet in great charismatic gatherings and experience little difficulty in fellowship though there may be wide theological differences. In many cases, those claiming to have gifts of the Spirit are not even born again and are members of churches where the gospel is ridiculed. However, they meet together on the basis of a *common experience.* Spiritual unity, however, cannot be attained with experience as a center. Paul argued forcefully that there must be sound doctrine in order to have proper spiritual unity (Eph. 4:1–16). Some old-line Pentecostals are concerned about the ecumenical tendencies of the new Pentecostals. Such a one, in decrying the ecumenical involvements of neo-Pentecostalists, noted, "The tongues experience seems to serve as a bridge over the chasm of theological difference" (J. R. Ensey, *The Pentecostal Herald,* November, 1972). Featured speakers at many charismatic conferences represent all portions of the theological spectrum. A Roman Catholic writer declares, "One of the richest fruits of this contemporary charismatic movement is the binding together of Christians of many denominations in the Spirit of Jesus. Episcopalians, Lutherans, Presbyterians, Methodists, Baptists, Disciples, Nazarenes, Brethren, as well as denominational Pentecostals, have become our very dear brothers and sisters in Christ, united by the baptism in the Holy Spirit" (Kevin Ranaghan, *Catholic Pentecostals,* 225). Nothing is said here as to whether or not all these persons are truly and Biblically born again. What is emphasized is that, supposedly, they have received the baptism in the Spirit.

As is indicated by the book just cited, Catholic Pentecostals are in increasing prominence in the charismatic movement. Most of them remain loyal to the Roman Catholic Church but claim to have received the baptism in the Spirit. Such experiences do not cause them to repudiate the apostasy of Catholicism, however. For instance, consider this report under the heading, "Pope Encourages Charismatic Renewal."

> Some 125 leaders of the Catholic charismatic renewal met near Rome October 9–13 to assess the growth of the charismatic movement within the Catholic Church and were warmly encouraged by Pope Paul VI. . . . The rapid growth of the Catholic charismatic renewal . . . is one of the extraordinary phenomena of the Roman Catholic Church today. . . . The unusual characteristic of the Catholic groups is that they have not, by and large, caused disunity and disruptiveness, but have developed in harmony with ecclesiastical leadership. (News story, *Catholic Voice*)

Could it be possible for such a movement to be of God, cooperating as it does with the hierarchy of Romanism? Can movements so careless about theological truth be fostered by the Holy Spirit Who is the Spirit of truth?

The Charismatic Movement as an Attraction to Evangelicals

Unfortunately it is human nature to be impressed by important personalities and to be attracted thus to whatever they may believe or endorse. The charismatic movement in recent years has grown steadily in influence and has attracted to itself numbers of well-known persons in various walks of life. Such organizations as the Full Gospel Businessmen's Fellowship have taken full advantage of this and have heralded leading citizens who supposedly have received the baptism of the Spirit.

Books by the dozens roll from evangelical presses promoting the charismatic movement. David Wilkerson struck the popular imagination and made inroads for charismatic doctrine in his best-selling book, *The Cross and the Switchblade.* More recently Corrie ten Boom, author of *The Hiding Place,* has been a speaker at charismatic rallies. The Logos International publishers are promoters of this position; Bethany Fellowship is as well. Creation House in Illinois and Fleming Revell in New Jersey are both helping to promote the "renewal."

There is a growing spirit of appeasement abroad among many evangelicals, particularly new evangelicals. Such a spirit characterizes Clark Pinnock and Grant Osborne in their article, "A Truce Proposal for the Tongues Controversy" (*Christianity Today,* 6 ff.). Their solution is given at the end of the article in the words of A. B. Simpson, founder of the Christian Missionary Alliance who wrote:

> We believe the Scripture teaching to be that the gift of tongues is one of the gifts of the Spirit, and that it may be present in the normal Christian assembly as a sovereign bestowal of the Holy Spirit upon such as he wills. We do not believe that there is any Scriptural evidence for the teaching that speaking in tongues is the sign of having been filled with the Spirit, nor do we believe that it is the plan of God that all Christians should possess the gift of tongues. . . . The attitude toward the gift of tongues held by pastor and people should be "Seek not, forbid not." (quoted in the *Alliance Witness,* 19)

Hal Lindsey, popular author, in his book *Satan Is Alive and Well on Planet Earth,* has declared that tongues-speaking is possible. Russell Hitt, editor of *Eternity* magazine, repented of his earlier-expressed opinion that the "new Pentecostalism" would go away, and wrote as follows:

> I have come to the position that it is a spiritual phenomenon, being used of God, very dramatically in some quarters. It is plainly bringing new life and

> virility to denominations long since pronounced dead or apostate by many evangelicals. Thousands have been ushered into the kingdom of God and others have received a new enduement of power despite the theological questions this raises. ("A Second Look At the New Pentecostalism," *Eternity,* 12 ff.)

Yes, it certainly does raise some theological questions and we would be wiser to explore these than to focus on the experiences of "thousands" who allegedly have been swept into God's kingdom.

The Charismatic Movement as a Foe of Biblical Separation

God's command for true believers to separate themselves from those who hold false doctrine still stands: "Wherefore come out from among them, and be ye separate, saith the Lord, and touch not the unclean thing; and I will receive you" (2 Cor. 6:17). Modern charismatics, however, glory in the fact that their shared experience of speaking in tongues transcends all denominational and practically all theological boundaries. They view such unfettered fellowship as part of the great "movement of God." What difference does it make whether a person believes in the verbal inspiration of Scripture, in the full deity of Christ, in the lost condition of man, or in the personal new birth? What difference does it make if a person is supporting the apostate program of a liberal denomination? If he or she has been "baptized in the Spirit" and is speaking in tongues, this is the most important matter.

To fellowship with people who deny or question great truths of God's Word is wrong. To justify such fellowship upon the basis of a common religious experience is no less wrong. It seems clear that the Pentecostal experience, the charismatic emphasis, is becoming a significant factor in the development of an ecumenical mood among many evangelicals. This mood bodes no good for the future testimony of Christ's churches. It will only serve to weaken their witness and to dilute it by unscriptural alignments.

The Charismatic Movement as a Disrupter of Local Churches

Much heartbreak and conflict has resulted in many local churches because of the infiltration of charismatic teaching. Generally speaking, it is difficult for persons who think they have received the "baptism in the Spirit" to keep quiet about it. In fact, they are encouraged to spread the "good news" and to tell neighbors and friends what has happened to them. When this is done within the context of a local church, it can divide the congregation. The writer was recently in a large midwestern city and inquired of a local pastor as to the status of a well-known church in that area. The sad tale was told. The pastor of the church had "received the gift of tongues." He began seeking to indoctrinate the people. Opposition arose, the church was disrupted, and the pastor left with a group to establish another congregation. Such stories could be repeated many times. Churches that have stood for the truth for years have been either captured and taken over by charismatics, or their ministry has been crippled because of their persistence in promoting their doctrinal peculiarities.

The Charismatic Movement as an Enigma to Believers

How do you explain the fact that some people seem to speak in tongues? This question is frequently encountered in discussions with believers. Keep several things in mind in facing the problem of the current charismatic movement.

In the first place, the phenomenon of tongues is not unique to Christianity. The fact that someone has spoken in tongues does not mean that he is a superior Christian, nor does it even suppose that he is a Christian at all. Certainly it does not require that the origin of his tongues-speaking be the Lord. The ancient Greeks had tongues-speakers as Plutarch and others record. Voodoo priests sometimes speak in tongues as do devotees of other pagan religions.

Also, most modern tongues-speaking is not spontaneous in nature. The New Testament accounts emphasize the spontaneity and supernaturalness of the gift when it was manifested in the early church. However, modern authors such as John P. Kildahl have underscored the fact that tongues-speaking is a learned skill (*The Psychology of Speaking In Tongues,* 74). Lest one be accused of undue bias against charismatics, the same truth can be found in a book by one of their own. Larry Christenson, a leading charismatic, details for his readers how they may begin to speak in tongues, outlining the steps to follow and declaring that if the seeker just starts talking and keeps talking in faith, the Spirit will shape his sounds into a language (*Speaking in Tongues,* 130). An utterance such as this that calls for concentration and practice can hardly be said to be the Biblical gift of tongues.

Probably most of what currently passes as the "gift of tongues" could be characterized as verbal utterances that are psychologically induced. Charles Smith has an excellent discussion of the psychology of tongues (*Tongues in Biblical Perspective,* 93–128). After analyzing various psychological factors that may be involved in some tongues-speaking, Smith enumerates several reasons why the gift of tongues has become so popular in modern times. Among those that he lists are: insecurity, spiritual hunger not satisfied in the modern church, a secularized society, and the generally impersonal nature of modern life.

Nor should the possibility of demonic control be overlooked. While a person should rightfully hesitate to attribute all tongues-speaking to demonic power, it is nevertheless a very real fact that, when humans relinquish control of their faculties, demons may seize them. The powers of darkness like nothing better than to imitate divine power, seeking thereby to lead people astray. Christians need to remember that just because a thing is marvelous, unusual, or seemingly unexplainable to man's mind does not mean that the thing in question is divine in origin. The coming emissaries of

Satan during the tribulation period will startle the world with extraordinary exploits (2 Thess. 2:9; Rev. 13:11–14).

❖

Ecclesiastical Confusion in the 21st Century

Dr. Pickering said the movement that promotes the sign gifts also promotes ecumenical activity that breaks down the God-ordained separation of true believers from those who are leaders in groups that do not clearly teach salvation by grace alone through faith alone in Christ alone. Here is a recent example of this ecclesiastical confusion.

Roman Catholic Cardinal Walter Kasper states:

> A practical consequence of this is the charismatic movement, through which the Pentecostal movement found its way into the Catholic Church. This movement is characterized by expressions of informal spontaneity, emotionality, and individuality in relation to experience. Admittedly, this sometimes leads to subjectivism, which comes into conflict with the objective nature of the liturgy. The charismatic movement within the Catholic Church has facilitated dialogue with the Pentecostal movements outside the Catholic Church. But in contrast to the Pentecostals, the Catholic charismatic movement remains within the sacramental and institutional structure of the Church; it therefore has the possibility of having a stimulating effect in the Church herself. ("Current Problems in Ecumenical Theology," http://www.ctinquiry.org/publications/reflections_volume_6/kasper.htm [accessed September 22, 2006])

Conclusion

In light of the testimony of Scripture it can and should be said: the modern charismatic movement is not of God. No doubt within it are true, though deluded, believers. God, however, is not bestowing the gift of tongues today. Those who claim to speak in tongues are not exercising a divine gift.

Genuine spiritual gifts are being bestowed upon true believers today. These spiritual gifts are very precious and are vital to the fulfillment of God's purposes in this age. Rather than seeking nonexistent gifts, believers should discover the gifts God has bestowed upon them and use these in the power of His Spirit to the upbuilding and edification of the Body of Christ.

Bibliography

Books

Brumback, Carl. *What Meaneth This?* Springfield, MO: Gospel Publishing House, 1947.

Burgess, Stanley M., ed. *The New International Dictionary of Pentecostal and Charismatic Movements,* rev. and exp. edition. Grand Rapids: Zondervan, 2002.

Christenson, Larry. *Speaking in Tongues.* Minneapolis: Dimension Books, 1968.

Geisler, Norman. *Signs and Wonders.* Wheaton, IL: Tyndale House, 1988.

Gromacki, Robert. *The Modern Tongues Movement.* Philadelphia: Presbyterian and Reformed, 1967.

Grudem, Wayne, ed. *Are Miraculous Gifts for Today? Four Views.* Grand Rapids: Zondervan, 1996.

Grudem, Wayne. *The Gift of Prophecy in the New Testament and Today.* Westchester, IL: Crossway Publishers, 1988.

Hoekema, Anthony. *What about Tongue Speaking?* Grand Rapids: Wm. B. Eerdmans Publishing, 1966.

Hodge, Charles. *Commentary on the Second Epistle to the Corinthians.* Grand Rapids: Wm. B. Eerdmans, n.d.

Jackson, Bill. *The Quest for the Radical Middle.* Cape Town, South Africa: Vineyard International Publishing, 1999.

Jorstad, Erling, ed. *The Holy Spirit in Today's Church.* Nashville: Abingdon Press, 1973.

Kelsey, Morton. *Encounter with God: A Theology of Christian Experience.* Minneapolis: Bethany Fellowship, 1972.

Kildahl, John P. *The Psychology of Speaking in Tongues.* New York: Harper and Row, 1972.

Lightner, Robert. *Speaking in Tongues and Divine Healing.* Schaumburg, IL: Regular Baptist Press, 1965.

McConnell, D. R. *A Different Gospel,* updated ed. Peabody, MS: Hendrickson Publishers, 1995.

Mills, Watson, ed. *Speaking in Tongues: Let's Talk about It.* Waco, TX: Word Books, 1973.

Patterson, Bob E., "Catholic Pentecostals," *Speaking in Tongues: Let's Talk about It.* Watson Mills, ed. Waco, TX: Word Books, 1973.

Ranaghan, Kevin and Dorothy. *Catholic Pentecostals.* New York: Paulist Press, 1969.

Ryrie, Charles. *The Holy Spirit.* Chicago: Moody Press, 1965.

Smith, Charles. *Tongues in Biblical Perspective.* Winona Lake, IN: BMH Books, 1973.

Storms, C. Samuel. *Are Miraculous Gifts for Today? Four Views.* Wayne Grudem, ed. Grand Rapids: Zondervan, 1996.

Unger, Merrill. *New Testament Teaching on Tongues.* Grand Rapids: Kregel Publications, 1971.

Walvoord, John F. *The Holy Spirit.* Findlay, OH: Dunham Publishing, 1958.

Wimber, John. *Power Evangelism.* San Francisco: Harper and Row, 1986.

Wright, Eric E. *Strange Fire?* Durham, England: Evangelical Press, 1996.

Magazines

Ensey, J. R. *The Pentecostal Herald* (November 1972).

Gundry, Stanley. "Facing the Issue of Tongues." *Moody Monthly* (October 1973): 96.

Hanegraaf, Hank. "The Counterfeit Revival, Part One: Rodney Howard-Browne and the Toronto Blessing." *Christian Research Journal* (July–August 1997): 8–18.

Hanegraaf, Hank. "The Counterfeit Revival, Part Three: Separating Fact from Fabrication on the Pensacola Outpouring." *Christian Research Journal* (November–December 1997): 11–20, 42.

Hitt, Russell. "A Second Look At the New Pentecostalism." *Eternity* (March 1976).

Hodges, Zane. "The Purpose of Tongues." *Bibliotheca Sacra* (July–September 1963): 228.

Houghton, Myron J. "A Reexamination of 1 Corinthians 13:8–13." *Bibliotheca Sacra* (July–September 1996): 344–356.

McLean, John A. "Did Jesus Correct the Disciples' View of the Kingdom?" *Bibliotheca Sacra* (April–June 1994): 215–227.

Pinnock, Clark and Grant Osborne. "A Truce Proposal for the Tongues Controversy." *Christianity Today* (October 8, 1971).

"Pope Encourages Charismatic Renewal." *Catholic Voice* (November 7, 1973).

Thomas, Robert L. "Prophecy Rediscovered? A Review of The Gift of Prophecy in the New Testament and Today." *Bibliotheca Sacra* (January–March 1992): 83–96.